ISTANBUL:
A TO Z

BY MAHVASH FAHD

First Edition, 2018

Copyright 2018 Istanbul: A to Z

Written by Mahvash Fahd
Gifted Kids Books
www.giftedkidsbooks.com

ISBN-13: 978-0692082300 (Gifted Kids Books)
ISBN-10:0692082301

Layout by Reyhana Ismail
www.reyoflightdesign.com

All rights reserved. No part of this publication may be reproduced in any language, stored in any retrieval system or transmitted in any form or by any means - electronic, mechanical, photocopying, recording or otherwise - without the express permission of the copyright owner.

Credits: Photographs & images are protected by copyright law. Resale or use of any images of this book is prohibited. Images © / Adobe Stock

Merhaba! Welcome to Istanbul: A to Z!

Who is this book meant for?
- Children learning the English alphabet
- Older children or adults, who wish to learn some of the famous landmarks in Istanbul and some basic Turkish words.
- Visitors to Istanbul who hope to remember some of the places they visited along with some basic Turkish words they are sure to pick up during their trip!

This book contains both English and Turkish words. Some words are in English, to provide a sense of familiarity to English speakers (e.g. cat, corn, chestnuts). Other words are in Turkish, as you would see them in print while you are in Turkey. Translations have been provided when the meaning of some Turkish words may not be clear.

The letters Q, W, and X do not exist in the Turkish language and have therefore been omitted from this book. Moreover, for the sake of simplicity, certain Turkish letters have been replaced by their closest equivalents in the English alphabet e.g. the letters, ü, ç, and ş have been replaced by u, c, and s. As a Turkish friend pointed out to me, such spellings of Turkish words are common "when Turks use a regular qwerty keyboard without the Turkish letters" (Thank you Hatice!).

Another point worth mentioning is that many of the words and landmarks in the book are known by additional names locally. For simplicity, typically only one name is depicted in the book. For instance, Constantine's Column is also known as the Burnt Stone.

I hope you enjoy your visit to Istanbul through the pages of this book!

Ataturk Airport

Aa

Adana kebab

Istanbul Archaeology Museum

Ayran (yoghurt drink)

Anadolu Hisari Fortress

Akide (candy)

Bb

Blue Mosque

Basilica Cistern

Bosphorus Bridge

Borek (savory pastry)

Biber (pepper)

Beylerbeyi Palace

Balik ekmek (fish sandwich)

Bayan (woman)

Baklava (dessert pastry)

Bay (man)

Cc

Constantine's Column

Cats

Calligraphy

Carpet

Cruise

Chestnuts

Ciragan Palace

Corn

Cay (tea)

Chora Church

Cikis (exit)

Corba (soup)

Dolmabahce Palace

Dd

Dervish

Dondurma (ice cream)

Doner (rotisserie meat)

Ee

Emirgan Park

Eminonu pier

Eczane (pharmacy)

Ekmek (bread)

Eyup Mosque

Ff

Fatih Mosque

Figs

Gg

Gulhane Park

Grand Bazaar

Galata Tower

Golden Horn Bay

Hh

Hammam (Turkish bath)

Hagia Sophia

Hippodrome

Ii

Istiklal Street

Iskender kebab

Iznik pottery

Jj

Jewelry

Janissary armor

Kk

Kurus (cent)

Kahve (coffee)

Kabatas Pier and Mosque

Kunefe (cheese dessert)

Kahvalti (breakfast)

Kadayif (dessert)

Ll

Lanterns

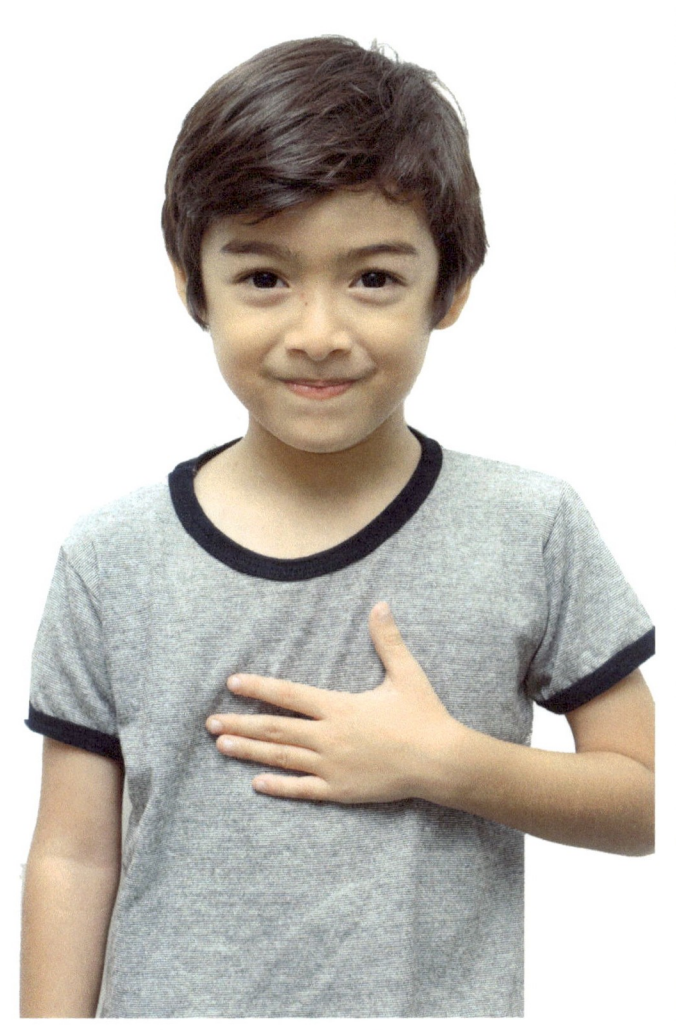
Lutfen (please)

Lokanta (restaurant)

Lira

Lahmacun (pizza)

Leander's Tower (Maiden's Tower)

Lokma (dessert)

Mm

Menemen (scrambled eggs)

Mimar Sinan

Miniaturk

Merhaba (hello)

Nn

New Mosque (Yeni Camii)

Oo

Ottoman Coat of Arms

Ortakoy Mosque

Obelisk of Theodosius (Egyptian Obelisk)

Pp

Patriarchate

Pierre Loti Hill

Pilav (rice)

Peynir (cheese)

Qq
The letter Q does not exist in the Turkish language

Rr

Rumelihisarı Fortress

Rustum Pasha Mosque

Ss

Simitci (simit vendor)

Simit (pretzel)

Sahlep (milk drink)

Spice Bazaar

Suleymaniye Mosque

Tt

Tughra (seal)

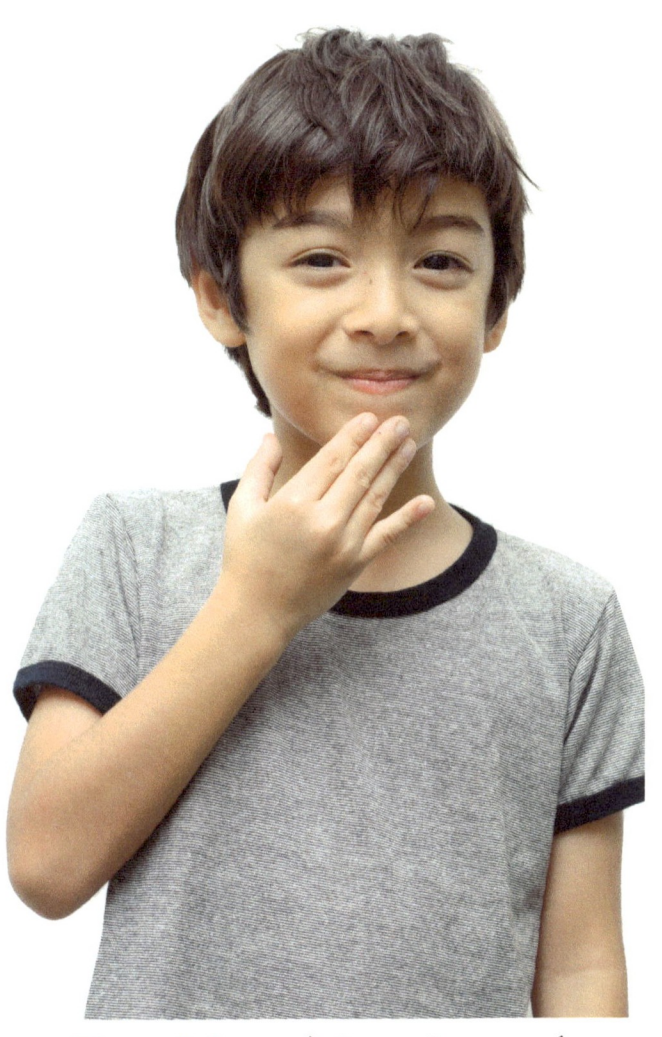
Tesekkur (thank you)

Taksim Square

Tavuk (chicken)

Turkish and Islamic Arts Museum

Turkish Delight

Topkapi Palace

Taksi (Taxi)

Uu

Universite (University)

Uskudar

Ww Xx

The letters W and X do not exist in the Turkish language

Valens Aqueduct

Vv

Visne suyu (cherry juice)

Yy

Yalis (mansions along the Bosphorus)

Yemek (food)

Zz

Zerde (sweet rice)

Ziyaret (visit)

www.ingramcontent.com/pod-product-compliance
Lightning Source LLC
Chambersburg PA
CBHW041228040426
42444CB00002B/96